PORTFOLIO H

METROPOLITAN SEMINARS IN ART

Great Periods in Painting

PORTFOLIO H

The War of Illusions: CLASSICISM VS. ROMANTICISM

BY JOHN CANADAY

ART EDITOR AND CRITIC
THE NEW YORK TIMES

THE METROPOLITAN MUSEUM OF ART

THE WAR OF ILLUSIONS

Classicism vs. Romanticism

THE FRENCH Revolution was born of a combination of high philosophical idealism on one hand and on the other the desperate necessity to pull together a disintegrating nation. The idealism had to do with the dignity of the human being and man's rights as an individual. Both of these ideals were violated in the most appalling ways in the years that followed the first shock of revolution in 1789. As France careened through the years of the Terror, no man's neck was safe from the guillotine, men were leaders of the state one day and under sentence of death the next, a puzzled little shopkeeper might be put to death for holding a few candles that had been government property, friends turned on friends to save themselves but lost their own heads in the process, and liberty, equality, and fraternity came to mean chaos, revenge, and universal peril.

In these ghastly years the painter Jacques Louis David (1748–1825) became a power in the Revolutionary Convention and voted for the death of his former patron, Louis XVI, an action for which his wife left him and for which some of his friends never forgave him. However, some historians defend David with the argument that he could not have done otherwise without giving the lie to the principles he had expounded in the paintings that had made him famous and powerful. These were his "stoic" paintings, *The Oath of the Horatii* (Portfolio G, *Figure 23*) and *Brutus* (Plate G 12), which had been interpreted as

declamations on the subject of the purification of France at whatever cost when the ideal of the liberty of the state was involved.

There is no evidence that casting his vote for the king's death or, in other cases, failing to intervene for friends under suspicion, caused David great anguish. And a chilling remark has come down to us, his "Is that all?" when an acquaintance reported to him that eighty people had been guillotined that day. But we know also that David cared for the aging Fragonard, who had once thrown a commission his way when David was poor and unknown.

David used to station himself along the route of the tumbrils to sketch the victims on their way to execution. The saddest of these drawings (*Figure 1*) shows the Widow Capet, as the Revolutionary Tribunal called the woman who had been Marie Antoinette, Queen of France. As queen she may have been as weak and vain and foolish as any young woman in history, but the Widow Capet is a heart-rending figure as David recorded her, bound hand and foot, every vestige of beauty gone, shattered by a frightful imprisonment, by illness, by the execution of her husband, by the loss of her child under circumstances whose abominations she could only guess, by the dissolution of the world she had known, by a scurrilous and venomous trial, by the loathing that poured out upon her from all of France. Yet she went to her death with a kind of numb courage, and people in the

Figure 1

antiquarian classicism of the stoic pictures toward a more democratic realism. In general his pictures of this period are not his most interesting ones, but they include one in which he rose above himself, his *Death of Marat* (*Figure 2*).

Marat, one of the powers of the new regime, was David's personal friend. He was stabbed by a woman named Charlotte Corday who, although a Revolutionary sympathizer, was outraged by the excesses of the Terror for which she held Marat among the guilty. Marat suffered from an eczema that forced him to spend days in a medicinal bath, which he rigged with pen, paper, and books at its side. Corday gained an audience in this makeshift office by saying that she had vital information to reveal, stabbed the helpless man, was arrested on the spot, and later guillotined.

As a subject for a painting, the episode had its ludicrous aspects and also offered every opportunity for wildly melodramatic treatment. But David distilled from it a picture

crowd who had no reason to feel anything but hatred and contempt for her wept and blessed her before the blade fell and put an end to a regime that had had its symbol as long as she was alive.

This was in 1793, when David, at forty-five, was not only a political power but the dictator of French art. As the official artist of the Revolution he painted numerous subjects connected with its history; he also organized and staged public ceremonies (some of which involved virtually every citizen of Paris), designed a new national habit for men that was supposed to replace pre-Revolutionary garb (it failed to catch on), and saw that all suggestions of royal association were removed from even such ordinary things as playing cards, which were redesigned to eliminate the knave, king, and queen. He saw that the Royal Academy was abolished, and its schools with it, these "in the name of justice, in the name of art, and above all in the name of youth." And he modified his own style away from the

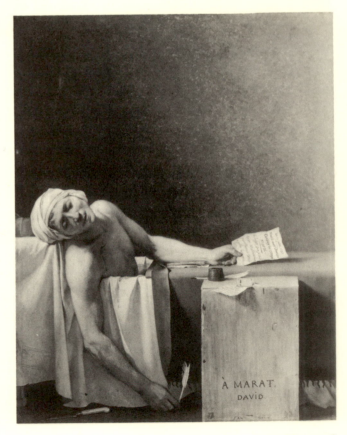

Figure 2

6

Figure 3

truly classical in its restraint, as well as one of his few works where his emotional response is not chastened into iciness.

David's great historical picture of the Revolution was to have been *The Oath of the Tennis Court*, showing the occasion when the deputies of the Third Estate, meeting in an indoor tennis court, swore not to disband until France had been given a constitution. The tremendous mass portrait was never finished because too many of the participants became suspect as the Revolution catapulted into the Terror. It was not long before David himself came under suspicion. He was an adherent of the Jacobin Robespierre, who was tried, condemned, and executed when his terrorist abuses became intolerable. David no doubt would have suffered likewise, but his trial was delayed, and in the interval following Robespierre's convic-

tion, passions cooled. There are eyewitness descriptions of David's discomfiture on the stand, of the dictator reduced to a sweating and mumbling supplicant. Unsympathetic biographers see David as an opportunistic turncoat who now denied Robespierre in claiming that he, David, had strung along only as a necessity to protect and serve the arts of France.

David's life was spared, and otherwise he did not fare badly. He was imprisoned, but in the Luxembourg Palace, one of several public buildings used to accommodate an overflow of prisoners. His so-called cell was a room with a view of the gardens, where their governess brought his children so that he could watch them at play. His friends and students kept him supplied with materials for whatever work he felt inclined to do.

7

Figure 4

David and Napoleon

During this agreeable incarceration, David made the first studies for what was to become his most important painting, with the possible exception of *The Oath of the Horatii*. *The Battle of the Romans and the Sabines* (*Figure 3*) shows the woman Hersilia throwing herself between Romulus and her Sabine father, Tatius, to stop the carnage as the Sabine men battle the Romans to recover their abducted women. Nominally the scene is one of violence and confusion. But David had conceived *The Sabines* as a return to purely classical style, in what he imagined to be a Greek manner, and he crystallized the action into a static composition which is, in truth, altogether artificial in effect, almost tinny in its gloss, and certainly more elegant, less forceful, than the stoic pictures. For Greek purity we find an imposed formula that draws only superficially on Greek forms; for Greek calm, a frozen rigidity; for Greek ideal beauty an inflexible figure type of

physically perfected beings who henceforth were to become the stock-in-trade of the revived Academy (without the hateful prefix "Royal") and the official schools that were revived with it.

David's imprisonment was of short duration. Upon his release he withdrew from politics, doing some portraits and working at *The Sabines* on a canvas seventeen feet wide. After completing it in 1799, he put it on exhibition, charging an admission fee. His luck was uncanny; again he was the sensation of Paris, again his picture was given a political interpretation, and again he was lifted to dictatorship.

How he happened to choose the subject of *The Sabines* is not certainly known. Perhaps it simply appealed to him as a subject for a composition recalling his earlier classical successes and a relief from the historical Revolutionary pictures that had occupied him for several years. One theory is that the picture was begun as a tribute to his wife, who had returned to him in his trouble. But politically it was interpreted as an allegory of the moment. Napoleon had come into power, and was solving the conflicts of liberty by imposing a new totalitarianism. The woman Hersilia was now seen as a symbol of France throwing herself between rival factions to end the sanguinary conflicts that had torn the country since 1789. David accepted this interpretation, and when Napoleon saw *The Sabines*, he recognized in the ex-royalist protegé and the ex-Revolutionary disciple precisely the man to enter a third incarnation as the propagandist of empire.

Under Napoleon, David's dictatorial powers reached their peak. The emperor's idea was to surround himself with all the appurtenances of a Caesar. Just as the rococo style had set the proper ambiance for Madame de Pompadour, now neoclassicism set it for Napoleon. His church, the Madeleine, was by his order a pure classical temple; his Arc de Triomphe is an enlargement of Roman models. Furniture and decoration became as Roman and Greek as archaeology—with concessions to contemporary life—could make them, and the fashionable women of Paris contracted pneumonia in gauzy classical gowns of bacchantes and goddesses.

David's portrait of Madame Récamier (Plate H1), one of the beauties of the day, has become the epitome of the classical revival styles in France. The beauteous charmer reclines in what might be mistaken for a theatrical costume in a classical drama, but was in fact a modish gown, upon a couch of a design that has borne her name ever since, in repetitions and variations by the thousand, not only in France but in every other country of Europe and even in America. The picture is not quite finished, and hence does not have the merciless polish of most of David's work; it gains in freshness because the touch of his brush is still apparent. He stopped work on it after a disagreement with the lady. Her hair was raven black and she was proud of it, but David insisted upon making it light brown to harmonize with his general color scheme and to follow the classical formula by which all hair was blond or reddish.

David had accepted the commission in the first place as a concession to a woman from whom few men were able to withhold a favor. Under Napoleon he was busy with a series of commissions that would have taxed the energies of even a younger man. The most gargantuan assignment was a series of four canvases that would have totaled some 2,000 square feet, apotheosizing the emperor. Only two were finished; the first of them, *The Coronation (Figure 4)*, is an admirable but somewhat wearing recreation of the point during Napoleon's coronation when the empress, Josephine, receives the crown from her husband. Napoleon wears the one he had received from the Pope just before; he preferred to have the later episode of the ceremony pictured be-

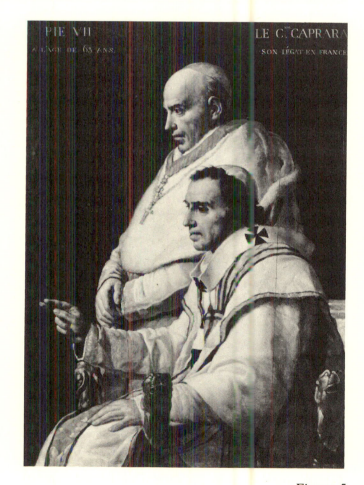

Figure 5

cause he had knelt before the pope to receive his crown (although he had placed it on his own head) and did not want to go down to posterity shown at any man's feet.

For *The Coronation* David had a band of assistants, but he sketched in all the portraits, completed the major ones with his own hand, and did detailed studies of the most important ones. A double portrait of the Pope and his Legate, the Cardinal Caprara, an element of *The Coronation* that David repeated as an independent picture (*Figure 5*), indicates the detailed fidelity of style; for again, as in the Revolutionary pictures, David was asked to modify his classical ideal in creating a factual record. *The Coronation* is as much a document as it is a painting; yet as a work of art in its own right it is an impressive organization of material that offered very little flexibility, since the scene had to be recreated just as it had been staged. David unified the picture less by the usual devices of line and mass and color than by the only one he was free to adjust, light. He constructed a scale model, with costumed figures, as a kind of miniature stage upon which he directed light from artificial sources for the double purpose of unifying all the figures in a logical relationship, and focusing attention on the principal ones.

It would seem that David's career could not

Archives Photographiques, Paris

Figure 6

enter another phase, after so many, but there was still one more. When Napoleon tottered, David either misjudged the political future or, for once, remained steadfast to a master. He signed petitions which, after the debacle, made it wise for him to flee the country. He was wealthy enough to live comfortably in Brussels where, at a distance, he remained the most powerful force in French painting, while he continued to occupy himself with a few commissions and with painting for his own pleasure. In the grace, even the sentiment, of its subject, his *Mars Disarmed by Venus and the Graces* (Plate A3), completed just before his death, relents somewhat from his usual disciplines and restrictions, but otherwise it remains a typical example of the technique and approach that made David the leader and the archetype of neoclassical painting.

David's conception of discipline and restriction as the basis of painting reduced the artist to a narrow range of expression. David himself said that the manner he had established was "too severe to please for long in France," and even among his most loyal followers this truth was apparent. Some of them, like Pierre Narcisse Guérin (1774–1833), followed his recipes yet ended with dry, unconvincing productions like *The Return of Marcus Sextus* (*Figure 6*). Others managed to be Davidian on the surface yet to go beyond Boucher in sugary sweetness, as one of David's favorite pupils, François Gérard (1770–1837), in his *Psyche Receiving the First Kiss from Cupid* (*Figure 7*). Yet in spite of such indications that Davidian classicism had run its course, the Academy continued to resist change until well into the second half of the century.

The Romantic Spirit

David's stoicism had had point before the Revolution, but the volcanic events thereafter hardly supported the basic concept of classical art, which is that of an underlying harmony in the world, in existence. The truest classical art, that of the Golden Age of Greece, grew out of a time that could legitimately conceive of this harmony. But in the years between David's *Horatii* and his *Mars Disarmed by Venus* France had flowed with her own blood, Napoleon had soaked the fields of Europe with more of this blood and with that of other nations, the country had known chaos, grandeur, defeat, and humiliation, had seen events magnificent, ignoble, fantastic, glorious, and abysmal. It had seen everything but order, had felt everything except serenity. The people of France and of Europe had passed through crisis after crisis, were parts of a world that changed from day to day, a world in which the individual felt lost, menaced, helpless against forces he could not control or, often, understand. The formulas of neoclassical art in such a world seemed not only limited but false. The answer to life was not to be found in them; people sought it elsewhere and hoped to find it in that vast complex of yearning, mysticism, dramatics, reflection, indulgence, and rebellion against authority that is called romanticism— a term, obviously, of rich and varied meaning.

Where classicism put its faith in the intellect, romanticism was pledged to the fulfillment of the heart's desires; where classicism insisted that the creative instinct must be subjected to rule, romanticism rejected every rule that might obstruct the full expression of self. Classicism was a way of thought; romanticism was a way of feeling, and it became a way of life.

Men became obsessed with their mortality, with the chanciness of fate. They were willing to risk disaster rather than risk unfulfillment. The unknown became more fascinating than the known, and the romantics sought far away places and exotic adventures because the world around them seemed frustrating or humdrum. Life was to be seized and devoured rather than examined and controlled. And always there was an undercurrent of melancholy, of foreboding, an awareness of sinister or indifferent forces that in the end must defeat man

Figure 7

unless, as an individual, he fulfilled himself through love, through the senses, through the emotions, through every experience—even the experiences of pain and sorrow—before the body that housed his spirit failed him or was destroyed.

The romantics found themselves (or at least searched for themselves) everywhere: in communion with nature; in the ruins of the past that spoke to them of lost loves and faded glories; in streets and garrets where they might find themselves through others like themselves; in alcohol and opium that transformed them for a while into the free spirits and hypersensitive beings they yearned to be; in passion and in religion. In the arts such feelings could not be expressed within the limits of Davidian dogma, nor in the similar classical forms of drama, poetry, and music. In all fields the romantics returned to old forms more sympathetic to their needs, or invented new ones to meet those needs.

11

Figure 8

Gros

The romantic spirit was so strong that it broke through in unexpected places, like a plant forcing its way through pavement. As a conspicuous example, the painter Antoine Jean Gros (1771–1835) was a dedicated follower of David, an officer in Napoleon's army, and his ardent worshiper. By intention and by effort Gros was a classical artist, but by temperament he was a romantic spirit. His idolatry of Napoleon was deeply emotional, and when he came to paint an incident of the Near Eastern campaign showing the general visiting the pesthouse in Jaffa, where stricken members of his troops were dying of the plague (*Figure 8*), Gros emotionalized the subject by unclassical contrasts of light and shadow, by dramatic color, and by emphasizing exotic elements. The locale was, of course, exotic. But as a

matter of factual accuracy, the hospital was an ordinary one, and Gros chose to paint, instead, a courtyard of mosquelike architecture. And the dying man, nude, upon his knees, who turns his eyes toward his general with his last strength, is a far departure from David's classically polished warriors. He is a man of flesh and blood and anguish.

Gros was unable to rein in his brush in David's way; yielding to temptation, he painted richly and freely, in character with his unquenchably romantic conceptions. At another pole of romantic feeling, that of melancholy revery, he painted Christine Boyer (Plate H2), the beautiful first wife of Lucien Bonaparte. In her classical dress she is posed in a romantically shadowed wood, beside the bank of a stream upon which a single rose is about to be borne beyond our sight. The picture is full of mysterious suggestions, of the tenderest responses to a subject that is all the more moving for violating the classical precept of completeness within itself. We are led in a dozen directions of speculation, of sentiment; looking at it, we know we, too, are romantics.

Gros would not admit that he was one. In his late middle age the romantic movement blasted through the classical fortress, which he tried to hold after David's exile. In his last pictures, trying to weed out his own romantic tendencies, to which the public had responded enthusiastically, Gros created only a shallow and pompous approximation of the grand manner. His last Salon picture was laughed at; he died a suicide in two feet of water.

It may seem absurd that any man, even one of Gros's known emotional instability, should be led to suicide even partly by conflicting theories of aesthetics. But it is difficult for us to realize the intensity of the romantic-classic conflict, a conflict not only of theories of art but of morals, politics, emotions, and religion.

The Revival of Christianity

Although it reached its culmination in France, the romantic revolt stirred early in Germany. The German Caspar David Friedrich (1774–1840) is virtually unknown in America except to students, and for that matter is neglected generally outside his own country. He was a painter whose work has been dogged by misfortune: some of his best paintings were destroyed by fire in 1931 while on exhibition in the Glass Palace in Berlin, and during the Second World War his most important works were stolen from German museums and have yet to be located, if they exist. One of these is his *Cloister Graveyard in the Snow* (*Figure 9*), a great romantic picture painted in 1810.

Figure 9

13

Friedrich discarded classical temples along with classical aesthetic concepts and painted the Gothic monuments that were at the time only beginning to be regarded as something other than monstrous violations of the classical spirit. Especially in ruins they spoke to him of the soul, of both its hopes and its

Figure 10

loneliness. He was attracted to Gothic architecture also because he thought of it as indigenously German, and the revitalization of German art was one goal of German romanticism. More strongly than any other factors, however, a return to Christianity inspired Friedrich and his fellow early romantics.

Eighteenth-century rationalist philosophy had denied Christianity, and the French Revolution had outlawed the church. German romanticism was an early return to faith in the non-rational, a trust that led sometimes to muzzy mysticism, sometimes, as in Friedrich and his friend Philipp Otto Runge (1777–

1810), to a return to Christianity as a religion of miracle and revelation, as it had been for the common man during the Middle Ages, and to a search for God as manifested in natural wonders.

Like much romantic art of the period, Runge's *Lily of Light* (*Figure 10*) is sentimental and obvious to contemporary eyes. But his *Rest on the Flight into Egypt* (Plate H3) is another story. The unquestioning faith that pervades the picture differentiates it from any religious pictures, except Blake's, painted since the early Renaissance. Like Friedrich, Runge saw nature as the supreme manifestation of God; the deep landscape in the *Rest on the Flight* was intended to be a mystical statement in terms of the familiar, as indeed it is. More obviously mystical is the tree whose foliage and branches flower suddenly into joyous infant angels, a more successful treatment of the same idea that is a bit mawkish in the *Lily of Light*.

Contributing most subtly to the air of the extraordinary and the wonderful in the *Rest on the Flight* is the least likely element, the ass that stands at the extreme left. Drawn in acute foreshortening, complicated by the oddly shaped saddle and the blanket draped over it, the silhouette of the ordinary beast becomes a shape of fantasy.

Runge died in his early thirties, and destroyed quantities of his work virtually on his deathbed. The *Rest on the Flight* is not quite finished, the canvas being bare in the extreme upper right. If Runge had lived, with Friedrich he might have brought to fruition an early movement in German art that was only partially realized. As it was, the movement tapered off in the work of the Nazarenes, a group of painters with semimonastic ideals who copied early religious art under the delusion that the spirit might be transmitted through the borrowed forms. German romantic painting flowered only as a second growth, later in the century, when the decisive battles had been fought in France.

Atala

The revival of Christianity played its part in one of the most curious paintings produced in France as the romantic spirit began to infiltrate, in disguise, the ranks of classicism. *The Entombment of Atala* (Plate H 4) by Anne Louis Girodet de Roucy Trioson (1767–1824) was painted in the same decade as the German pictures we have just seen, as well as David's *Coronation*. Girodet was an artist with a respectable classical reputation who continued to work at least superficially along the lines of academic formula. At first glance the beautiful dead maiden seems to be in classical garb, and her mourning lover could be a gladiator, although the presence of the monk is thus an anachronism. To explain all this, a short literary excursion is necessary.

In 1791, a young French aristocrat named François René de Chateaubriand (1768–1848) visited America. Girodet's windy-haired portrait (*Figure 11*) says a great deal about this romantic spirit who loathed the Revolution and Napoleon equally, who made Christianity fashionable in France with a treatise, *Le Génie du christianisme*, which was more of a revolt against the status quo than a return to religion. Chateaubriand was received by George Washington in Philadelphia, but his interest in America was in its wilderness and the savage Indians who, by Rousseauist ideas, were among the few noble human beings still to be found in a widely corrupted world.

In America Chateaubriand went as far as he could into the wilds. He certainly went into the territory that is now Ohio, and he visited Niagara Falls, then a majestic spectacle in all its natural grandeur. This was the America that fascinated all Europe, the gigantic and exotic world in which Indians still roamed. Like most tourists, Chateaubriand came prepared to see the country in terms of his preconception of it. What he saw was wonderful enough, but because he was a true romantic, what he imagined in retrospect was even more

Figure 11

fantastic. Here is his description of the scene along a river he calls the Meschacebé, which takes a moment to identify as the Mississippi:

The two banks of the Meschacebé present the most extraordinary picture. On the west bank, plains stretch away until lost in the distance, their rippling verdure receding until it mounts into the azure of the sky to vanish there. In these boundless prairies one sees troops of three or four thousand wild buffalo wandering. Sometimes a bison, full of years, breasts the current to make his bed on an island of the Meschacebé. With his forehead ornamented with two crescents, with his ancient matted beard, you would take him for the God of the River, throwing a satisfied glance upon the grandeur of his waves and the wild abundance of his shores.

Such is the scene on the left bank, but it changes on the opposite one, forming an admirable contrast with the first. Hanging over the flowing waters, gathered upon the boulders and upon the mountains, scattered in the valleys, trees of every form, of every color, of every fragrance, mixed and tangled with one another, mount into the air to heights

15

that tire the eye. Wild vines, begonias, gourds are interlaced at the foot of these trees, climb their trunks, cling to the extremity of their branches, leap from the maple to the tulip tree, from the tulip tree to the hibiscus, forming a thousand grottos, a thousand arches, a thousand porticos. Often, wandering from tree to tree, these vines traverse inlets of the river, across which they throw bridges of flowers. From the heart of this mass the magnolia lifts its immobile cone; surmounted by its great white roses it dominates all the forest, rivaled only by the palm waving its leafy fans alongside.

At the end of a vista one perceives bears, drunk upon grapes, staggering along the branches of young elms; caribous bathe in a lake; black squirrels play within the dense foliage; mocking birds and Virginia doves light upon the turf red with strawberries; green parrots with yellow beaks, crimson woodpeckers, fiery cardinals circle up to the top of the cypresses; humming birds glitter among the jasmine flowers, and serpents hiss suspended from the dome of the forest, swaying there like vines.

It is unlikely that Chateaubriand descended the Mississippi, although he liked to give the impression that he had done so. In any case he could not have seen two such bizarrely contrasting shores. The jungle he invented from hearsay and imagination is the setting for his short novel *Atala*, from which the above quotation was translated, the story of a half-breed girl and her Indian lover Chactas, a wildly romantic tale that would sound absurd in summary, full of grotesquely impossible incidents but full also of the passionate eloquence, the rich color, the escape into a never-never land of exoticism, and a preoccupation with personal emotionalism, that were to characterize the romantic movement within a few years. The novel had a tremendous vogue, and Girodet's *Entombment of Atala* illustrates its concluding episode.

The maiden Atala has killed herself as the result of an insoluble personal dilemma. In love with Chactas, as he with her, she is unable to marry him because her mother had taken a holy vow that the child would be dedicated to perpetual virginity. The monk who helps Chactas bury the dead maiden is a member of a Christian mission in the Florida jungles, serving as spiritual father to these Christianized Indians. Far-fetched, to say the least, the story fascinated a public that had had its fill of more rational fare. And in an odd connection its Christian elements had topical, rather than mystical, appeal since Napoleon's re-establishment of the Church had brought Christianity into fashionable favor in a way that had little to do with the more truly mystical and emotional Christianity of nascent romanticism in Germany.

Christianity, exoticism, emotionalism— these factors are synthesized in Girodet's picture to produce a prophetic hybrid, for the surface remains classical, in spite of the darkling shade and theatrical light that were to be exaggerated as emotive devices by the romantics, just as they had been by other painters we have seen in the seventeenth century. *The Entombment of Atala* like *Napoleon in the Pesthouse at Jaffe* is an expression, although a rather artificialized one, of the strength of romantic impulses even at a time when the classical mode enjoyed its greatest authority.

Géricault

In 1818, ten years after Girodet's picture was completed, the romantic rebellion came into the open with *The Raft of the Medusa* (*Figure 12*), by Théodore Géricault (1791–1824). We have seen this picture in a discussion of composition (Portfolio 6, Plate 71), commenting on the lunging force with which it builds across the canvas like a wave ready to break and topple, as opposed to David's neatly balanced seesaw arrangements. Caravaggio and Michelangelo, rather than Poussin and David, inspired it. Naturally, the picture was a scandal among conservative painters. The furor in the Salon of 1819 (the year after the picture was completed) had not been so great since David's exhibition of *The Oath of the Horatii*. The idea of devoting a picture of such scale (it is nearly twenty-four feet long) to a contemporary event involving not contemporary heroes, as in *The Coronation*, but common sailors, ran counter to every academic idea of the function of monumental painting. And, as with David's early pictures, political circumstances increased the excitement, although this time it was not necessary to hunt allegories.

logue hopefully gave the picture's title merely as "A Shipwreck," nobody was fooled and the public thronged to see it, first in Paris and then elsewhere when Géricault followed David's example and set it up for exhibition with an admission fee. Only a fraction of the thousands of people who saw *The Raft of the Medusa* came to see it because it was a work of art;

Figure 12

stances increased the excitement, although this time it was not necessary to hunt allegories.

The picture illustrated a current scandal: the French frigate *Medusa* had sunk in tropical waters; a raft had been improvised from parts of the ship; officers who had been towing this makeshift cut it adrift to save their own lives; by the time the raft was sighted only a handful of men had survived exposure, thirst, and cannibalism. The incident was used by the liberal party to attack the corruption of the party in power, and although the Salon cata-

nevertheless, it introduced a large public to romantic ideas in painting.

Géricault abandoned all pretense of classical purity and discretion. His paint was heavy and rich (sometimes, it must be admitted, rather coarsely and brutally applied, as the classicists objected). Light and shade were forced to their dramatic limits (sometimes beyond them into melodrama) and the refined and smoothly modeled features of the classical type, which had continued to serve Girodet for his "Indians" in *The Entombment of Atala*, were dis-

17

carded for rugged, irregular ones whose projections and concavities had nothing to do with ideal beauty but everything to do with the expression of human emotion. Instead of studying ancient sculpture, Géricault sketched in morgues (*Figure 13*) and madhouses, and watched men die in hospital wards. He is sometimes accused of morbid preoccupations, and the accusation may be justified. Nevertheless, his interest in abnormal states of mind was related to the interest of contemporary physicians in these states, which was the beginning of the serious study of insanity. It was also a logical extension of the romantic cultivation of sensibilities, the yearning to experience all emotions at full intensity, even beyond the limits accepted as the bounds of normality.

Ingres

When Géricault died, at thirty-three, as the result of a fall from a horse, the romantic banner was picked up by his younger friend Eugène Delacroix (1798–1863), who ultimately carried it to victory. His opponent in the classical camp was Jean Auguste Dominique Ingres (1780–1867), who inherited the leadership of the Academy after some early misunderstandings.

The contest between Ingres and Delacroix was bitter, and frequently came down to per-

sonal terms, at least on Ingres's part. The two men were identified as warring generals by a public that enjoyed the classic-romantic battle from the ringside seat of Paris. A popular cartoon (*Figure 14*) showed Ingres and Delacroix jousting in front of the Institute of France (the seat of the various Academies, including that of the fine arts). Ingres is armed with the tiny, pointed brush with which the precise and linear forms of classical painting were given their final polish, while Delacroix's lance is the broader, heavier brush of a painter who works more freely. (The academicians accused Delacroix of painting with "a drunken broom.")

The reader may want to place side by side, at this point, the Ingres and Delacroix plates from this Portfolio, Ingres's portrait of the painter Granet (Plate H 5) and his *Jupiter and Thetis* (Plate H 6), and Delacroix's *Arab Rider* (Plate H 7). These should be accompanied by three plates from preceding discussions: Ingres's *Madame Leblanc* (Portfolio 1, Plate 2), and two by Delacroix, *The Abduction of Rebecca* (Portfolio 6, Plate 72) and *Liberty Leading the People* (Portfolio 11, Plate 125). The miniature exhibition of classic-vs-romantic

should be understandable in the light of what we have just been saying. We will make a final point in what we have to say of these developments in France, with the idea of showing that the separation between classicism and romanticism could be a most arbitrary one, and was most arbitrary in the work of these two leaders. At the height of the conflict, the classical leader was at heart a romantic, although he never admitted it, and probably never recognized it. And the romantic forces were led by a man who regarded himself as the truest classicist of them all, in spite of his romantic partisanship.

Ingres was the favorite student of David. Before he was twenty he was entrusted with important details in the master's pictures; he executed the standing lamp that is so conspicuous in the portrait of Madame Récamier. A serious disagreement of some kind, never explained and never reconciled, separated master and student shortly after this, but Ingres continued to venerate David's tradition. He won the Prix de Rome with an expert classical composition, but his sponsors were not pleased with the direction his work then began to take.

Their disapproval centered on the beautiful portrait of Madame Rivière (*Figure 15*) exhibited in the Salon of 1806, an exquisitely designed composition of linear rhythms filled with the flowing sinuosity, the special combination of springy strength and languorous grace, that lifts Ingres above all other painters with the exception of Botticelli in this field. The academicians objected to the passages where knotted bunchings and intricate convolutions relieve by contrast the longer, simpler lines that, otherwise, might have been monotonous. They called the picture "Gothic," which they considered an epithet of opprobrium, a word that was to haunt Ingres all his life.

Ingres could not understand these objections; he was hurt and confused. Indeed the objections are hard to understand except in

Figure 15

terms of the narrowest kind of pedantry. In the following years, in Rome, Ingres somewhat modified his style. The portrait of Granet, shortly after that of Madame Rivière, was done under the influence of a new enthusiasm. Ingres had discovered Raphael, who was to be his god from then on, even above David and Poussin. The Granet portrait might be compared with Raphael's of Giuliano de' Medici (Portfolio 2, Plate 17). From Raphael Ingres has learned a more ornamental and more elegant disposition of silhouettes, and the linear arabesque defining these silhouettes is simpler than in the *Madame Rivière*, and stabler. The flowing lines of the open cape and its thrown-back collar are contrasted with the rectangular shape of the book Granet holds. The head with its curling locks is played against an eventless sky, and in the distance the buildings of the Academy, on the loveliest of the Roman hills, are not only a memento of time and place but serve by their smallness in the distance to increase the importance of the larger,

19

bolder silhouette of the handsome young man.

As the last work of his term of study in Rome, Ingres painted *Jupiter and Thetis*, illustrating a passage that we can still see marked in his copy of a French translation of *The Iliad* that he kept at his side. Thetis, a sea nymph, begs Jupiter to grant victory to the Trojans to avenge an insult to her son Achilles. The request is granted in spite of the fact that the god must thus incur the wrath of Juno (whose head appears with prophetic menace at the upper left border). Jupiter grants Thetis's request because he had at one time secretly loved her, and renounced his love. The passage Ingres marked translates thus:

> Thetis arose from the waves of the sea, and at the break of day rose through the immensity of the sky to Olympus. There she found him whose eye sees all the universe, the son of Saturn, seated far from the other gods on the highest summit of the mountain. She appeared before him and, with one hand upon his knees and lifting the other to his chin, she implored the monarch. But the god who commands the clouds answered nothing; he remained long in silence. Then this god of thunder let escape from his breast a profound sigh, and said, 'I promise you the satisfaction of your desires, and in pledge I accord you the sign of my sacred head.' Thus he spoke, and knit his black brows; the divine hair stirred upon the immortal head, and vast Olympus trembled, and Thetis, from the height of dazzling Olympus, threw herself again into the depths of the sea.

Jupiter and Thetis is one of Ingres's most personal works, one for which he kept a special affection all his life. In it he pushed to the extreme the distortions in linear patterns that appear so often in his early works, and that accounted for some of his early trouble with the Academy. (They are apparent in the unusual length of one arm in *Madame Rivière*.) *Jupiter and Thetis* was his last work under the regulation that required a Prix de Rome winner to complete one picture annually to send back to Paris. Because he was at the end of his term, perhaps he felt more free than usual to risk the hated cries of "Gothic" and to draw just as he pleased. The odd, long, swollen neck of the nymph, the almost serpentine arms flowering into tiny hands, the sudden complications of drapery—all these are played against the huge body of the god, of an awesome yet sensuous majesty.

Here, as in most of his best pictures, Ingres's deep sensuousness sets him apart equally from the frigidity of David and the merely titillating prettiness of such pseudo-Davidians as Gérard in *Psyche and Cupid*. Some critics harp on Ingres's "bourgeois vulgarity," disliking what they interpret as a hypocritically concealed sexuality. This could be true if we accept the premise of a shallow nature. But the more one sees of Ingres, the more one may realize that in spite of whatever controls he imposed upon himself he painted from profound emotional responses to his subjects. The pictures in which he attempts purely intellectual themes are failures. We have said that *Jupiter and Thetis* is an extremely personal expression. Like many of Ingres's best paintings it can be interpreted as a release of repressed passions, but it is a legitimate release, and it springs from one of the deepest sources of the creative impulse. Painting for Ingres was an emotional fulfillment, not an intellectual exercise or a means of philosophical dissertation. No other quality is more typical of romanticism, and thus Ingres, the defender of the classical, shares with the romantics, whom he loathed, the wellspring of their art.

Delacroix

On the other hand there was Delacroix, who created his tempestuous and technically romantic pictures intellectually and who by his own statement sought to generalize the entire range of human emotion. The poet and critic Baudelaire called Delacroix's work "a kind of remembrance of the greatness and native passion of the universal man." Universalization of this kind is a classical goal; it was because they sought a universal ideal rather than individual expression that the Greeks developed sets of standard features and standard bodily proportions that varied little from image to image. Unlike David, Delacroix refused to borrow these proportions in the expectation of acquiring with them the classical spirit that had generated them. Delacroix went instead to exotic and turbulent subjects, not for their picturesqueness but because they offered the widest range of strong emotions uncorrupted by the leveling humdrum of everyday life or the threadbareness of the classical legends as overworked by the academicians.

The orient supplied Delacroix with these subjects, just as it supplied picturesque material for battalions of other romantic artists, both painters and literary men. The determining experience of Delacroix's life was a trip to Morocco in 1832, when he was attached to a diplomatic mission at the request of its leader, young, aristocratic Count of Mornay, a friend of Delacroix's in the world where high society and upper Bohemia mingled in Paris. In Morocco the sultan opened all doors for the mission. Delacroix saw not only the lavish splendor of the palace and its entertainments, but traveled into the ordinarily dangerous countryside. He saw deserts, Arabs, native feasts, festivals, bizarre architecture, strange vegetation; he saw, smelled, tasted, felt, and heard the things of a world that he had only tried to imagine in the suave society and the silvery light of Paris. The hundreds of sketches he made in his Moroccan journal and the notes he scribbled there served him the rest of his life as a source book for his "remembrance of the greatness and native passion of the universal man." Whether he was painting Arab horsemen or a scene from a romance set in the Middle Ages, as he did in *The Abduction of Rebecca* (an episode from Sir Walter Scott's *Ivanhoe*), or an allegory as in *Liberty Leading the People* or a scene from the Bible as in *The Good Samaritan* (*Figure 16*), Delacroix was painting symbols in a vast emotional complex

Figure 16

to which the Moroccan experience gave form and color.

It remains true that some people find Delacroix a disappointing artist. Standing before his paintings they expect an emotional response that, somehow, fails to materialize. This is because we think of Delacroix first as the archromantic, and in pictures with such tempestuously emotional subjects we expect to find a personal expression. In Delacroix we do not. In the end his art is as impersonal as David's, or more so, and at least as calculated. That is why he called himself a true classicist: he sought universals, rather than personal particularities, and he sought them through the exercise of intellectual analysis, rather than the release of impulse.

But Delacroix's "truly classical" synthesis of universal passion could not be expressed in the neat forms of neoclassicism. At least he thought that it could not, and he went beyond Géricault in the use of the romantic devices we have discussed in connection with *The Raft of the Medusa*. Above all, he added to them the

21

concept of color as the expressive and structural foundation of painting. In Davidian painting, color was decorative rather than expressive; the sculptured forms, so to speak, were merely washed with smooth harmonious tints. Géricault is thought to have held to some idea of the emotional association of color in *The Raft of the Medusa*, using morbid and depressing hues, but the picture has darkened so that we can hardly tell what the original color was. In any case, the theory in all probability was not applied in much more than an elementary way.

Delacroix returned to the colorism of Watteau and more especially of Rubens, and with his "drunken broom" he often applied paint in broken strokes and unblended juxtapositions. This technique was to be carried further by the impressionists and then by Cézanne, with incalculable results in the twentieth century. When we come to our discussions of those topics we will have more to say about Delacroix as a colorist.

Ingres, Delacroix's senior by eighteen years, was an old man before he offered Delacroix his hand. In the meantime the Academy had forgiven Ingres the excesses of his "Gothic" youth. He became director of the École des Beaux Arts and also of the Academy in Rome. His life became a succession of official honors. So did Delacroix's, in a way. Although the Academy itself refused to recognize him until he was fifty-nine, he had influential friends who saw that he was awarded important official commissions, to the fury of the academic hacks who would ordinarily have received them.

In 1855, when Ingres was seventy-five and Delacroix fifty-seven, both men were given large retrospective exhibitions in the tremendous international Salon of that year. By that time a new school of painters had begun to storm the battlements. These were the realists, who found little to choose between classic and romantic idealism, since they regarded both as forms of a single illusion, the illusion that art

could nourish itself upon any substance other than life itself. So, by the middle of the century, the war of these illusions was terminating in a truce in the face of the common enemy.

England

English romantic expression may take excursions in various directions, but it keeps returning to an aspect of feeling that has been constant in English sensibility since the Middle Ages, the love of nature in its gentle, idyllic, and pastoral manifestations. We have already seen this expression in the painting of Gainsborough and Wilson. It continued uninterrupted, and strengthened, into the romantic decades of the nineteenth century and was brought to fruition in the landscapes of John Constable (1776–1837).

To Wilson's feeling for the poetic mood inherent in unexceptional bits of landscape, Constable added a perception of the dynamics of nature. His scudding clouds, twinkling leaves, flowing waters, bending grasses and shrubs are alive with the force that bursts seeds, pushes plants from the earth, sucks moisture into the air, forms it into clouds, and returns it to earth in showers. Rain sometimes darkens Constable's horizons, but more frequently it glitters after its fall on the freshened countryside, on the soft and darkened wood of fences and small bridges. Constable may paint the recesses of a glen or may take us toward the half-light of a cave of foliage, but the sky is the heart of his finest pictures, as in *Stoke-by-Nayland* (Plate H 8). These skies are not canopies; their union with fields and rivers and pools and streams is total. And the works of man that appear within this full and joyous harmony, whether cottages or cathedrals, seem to have grown in their places like trees or seem always to have been there, like outcroppings of stone.

The life that sparkles everywhere in a Constable comes in large part from his way of applying color in strokes juxtaposed against one another rather than blended into one another. In 1824 he exhibited a picture called *The Hay Wain* in the Paris Salon. Young Delacroix, who had been accepted with a smoothly painted canvas called *The Massacres of Scio*, was so excited by *The Hay Wain* that he repainted his own picture in the two weeks before the Salon opened, freeing his brush, loading his pigment, heightening his color, on Constable's model. The Salon that year centered around a smoothly conventional picture by Ingres (*The Vow of Louis XIII*) that re-established him in the Academy's favor, and *The Massacres of Scio*, which became a whipping boy for the pedants. Gros, who had heretofore sponsored Delacroix, called it "The Massacre of Painting." Yet *The Hay Wain* that had inspired Delacroix's new technique was accepted without excitement, an indication of the arbitrary and inconsistent basis of academic objections to romantic innovations.

In English painting there was no development quite comparable to the romantic-classic battle in France. Art had never been an instrument of national policy, and although Sir Joshua Reynolds formulated a set of pedantic rules and established the Royal Academy as their guardian, he did not manage to create a tradition of official painting like the one that had so powerfully affected French art since the time of Louis XIV. The classical style had its vogue in England as everywhere. But as practiced by, for instance, Benjamin West, who was one of its adherents in an irregular fashion, it served the international taste for the antique without becoming the expression of a moral code or a political chauvinism.

If the classical dogma was not insistent, neither were the early romantic expressions dramatized. In literature the story was different, with Lord Byron as the spectacular protagonist of a personal drama that corroborated the romanticism of his poetry. Yet he had little direct effect on English painting, although Delacroix so admired him that he painted *The Massacres of Scio* as a tribute to the Englishman's chivalric participation in the Greek war.

If Blake had been less eccentric he might have become the focus of an organized romantic revolt with his visionary art and his fulminations against "Sir Sloshua." As it was, he affected only a small circle of artists who gathered around him during the last ten years of his life, and this was without marked influence on subsequent painters. The most important of them was Samuel Palmer (1805–1881), an artist of highly individual romantic sensibilities when he was at his best, and a painter most inexplicably neglected today.

Palmer's *Coming from Evening Church* (Plate H9) was painted in 1830 when he was only twenty-five, three years after Blake's death. The young man's contact with Blake was brief, but Blake's influence is strong in this small picture, where much of his religious mysticism and something of his way of relating forms in a composition are apparent. But the ecstatic and sometimes grandiose tone of Blake's conceptions is replaced by a more idyllic pastoral mood, the typically English romanticism that was flowering in the poetry of Wordsworth.

If these comments suggest that *Coming from Evening Church* is nothing more than a neat synthesis of the virtues of Blake and Wordsworth, then they are misleading. The picture has its own character, distinct from the elements it shares with other painting and with poetry, a character determined by the combination of homely simplicity with formal mysticism that makes Palmer's early work unique in English painting. Palmer himself, within a few years, was to sacrifice this quality under the influence of Turner, whose titanic and spectacular effects he tried, without complete success, to approach (Portfolio 10, Plate 110).

Joseph Mallord William Turner (1775–1851) would be many people's candidate for the title of England's greatest painter, and few people would contest such pre-eminence for

Figure 17

him in English art since 1800. In his art, the English love of nature is expanded to grander dimensions; fields, clouds, streams, and sunlight are transmuted into abstract symbols of earth, air, water, and fire.

Turner began as an expert follower in the fine classical-decorative tradition of Poussin, Claude Lorrain, and other eighteenth-century descendants. But a comparison between his early *Dido Building Carthage* (*Figure 17*) and his late *Rain, Steam, and Speed* (*Figure 18*) shows the path he traveled. *Rain, Steam, and Speed* is a picture of a train crossing a bridge in mist, if you wish; it is also an abstraction in which matter is consumed, is translated into energy, suggesting at once the driving, charging force of a locomotive and the fusion of elemental forces of nature. We have already seen Turner's *Burning of the Houses of Parliament* (Portfolio 4, Plate 45), which also supplied him with a perfect subject, an exciting event, a

historical fact, that could serve as a point of departure for a cosmic spectacle.

Turner's landscapes and seascapes were ordinarily of subjects offering possibilities for similar translations—storms, blazing sunsets, mountains, waterfalls, and wild vistas. The less these pictures are regarded as landscapes (or seascapes) and the more they are regarded as abstract expressions of natural forces, the more meaningful they become. For this reason *Interior at Petworth* (Plate H 10) is particularly interesting, since the nominal subject has virtually nothing to do with the painting's effect. The canvas is a fiery, molten mass of color. If we try to find a subject in it we would be more likely to think first of a forge or a crucible than of a fine English house. Actually, the picture is one of Turner's many sketches and paintings done as personal souvenirs of his visits to Petworth House, the home of Lord Egremont. We may discover in it classical

24

archways and cornices, mirrors and paintings and sculpture around the walls, furniture, cloaks, and carpets in disarray. Yet these details are beside the point in a painting that is a fantasy of bursting light and glowing matter through which, with contrasting delicacy and humor rare in Turner, little dogs scamper.

The Pre-Raphaelites

Turner's last years at mid-century (he died in 1851 at the age of seventy-six) coincided with the beginnings of a romantic group called the Pre-Raphaelite Brotherhood, formed in 1848. The Pre-Raphaelites were England's first, and only important, organized rebels in the arts. Rather late in the game, they adopted the religious revivalism that had appeared in German art half a century before, and the combination of world-weariness and search for the exotic that was already threadbare in France. But to these they added their own revolt against the vulgarity and commercialism of the machine age, with the critic John Ruskin (who as a youth had been the first writer to discern Turner's power) as their spokesman.

There were good grounds for this revolt. England in her industrial prosperity was indeed guilty of the aesthetic horrors, the social abuses, and the intellectual smugness that were the worst aspects of the Victorian age. The Pre-Raphaelites were appalled, but unfortunately they sought a solution in the wrong direction: instead of going forward on the basis of the times' potential for good, they retreated into the past, escaping into the

Figure 18

25

Middle Ages as they imagined them to have been, surrounding themselves with a protective cloak of sentimentalism, and making the double mistake of pitying themselves and imagining themselves too good for the world around them.

The result was that they cut themselves off

the age of craftsmanship to the age of the machine. As used in the decorative arts, the machine was merely debasing designs borrowed from the past. The Pre-Raphaelites set about reviving hand crafts, to the point of doing their own weaving and cabinetmaking. Their mistake was in failing to see that hand

Figure 19

from vital intellectual and spiritual nourishment in all directions. Misunderstanding the Middle Ages, which they thought of as a halcyon time when everything was good, beautiful, and pure, they were denied even vicarious sustenance from the vitality of the Age of Faith. And rejecting the peculiar vigor and the fresh discoveries of their own time, whatever its faults, they were left with nothing to feed upon except negative values.

The one major contribution of the Pre-Raphaelites was that they called attention to evils that were inherent in the transition from

crafts could no longer supply needed objects for a crowded and acquisitive world. In addition, by their return to medieval designs, they revived the past rather than revitalized the present.

They chose the name Pre-Raphaelite in admiration of the artists of the late Middle Ages and particularly the early Italian Renaissance, with Benozzo Gozzoli and Botticelli in their hierarchy of idols. In imitating the styles of these painters the Pre-Raphaelites cut themselves off from the tradition of exuberant brushwork that Constable and Turner had established in the first half of the century, and thus they left to the French impressionists (who were soon to be at work) the development of a great modern movement that might have been their own.

Pre-Raphaelitism was a literary movement as well as one in painting and decoration. Among the founding members, Dante Gabriel Rossetti (1828–1882) is somewhat more sympathetically regarded these days as a poet than as a painter. His friend, William Morris (1834–1896), the finest decorative craftsman of the group, was a poet of merit far beyond his typically sentimental Pre-Raphaelite pictures.

Oddly, today the Pre-Raphaelites seem little different from the painters against whom they revolted, except for a hyperaestheticism that is not always agreeable. *Ophelia* (*Figure 19*), although by a nominally Pre-Raphaelite painter, John Everett Millais (1829–1896), has all the elements of popular appeal that were being cultivated by the academicians: expert painting of almost illusionistic realism; attractive details of flowers and costume, as well as a pretty girl; and a gold-plated cultural subject in Shakespeare's tragic heroine. Millais painted *Ophelia* in 1852, four years after the founding of the Brotherhood, and in the following year he was elected to the Royal Academy. This was a success for him, but in a way it was a defeat for the Brotherhood; Rossetti, as the typical founding member, was dedicated to revolt, Bohemianism, and poverty, all of which were denied by academic success. The Pre-Raphaelites soon enjoyed such a vogue that they constituted, for a generation, a little Academy among themselves.

The most prominent leader of the group of slightly younger men who joined the movement soon after its founding was Edward Burne-Jones (1833–1898), a close follower of Rossetti and for a long time a fellow worker in the crafts of tapestry and stained glass with William Morris. Burne-Jones seems the most satisfying of the Pre-Raphaelites today, for he studied the Middle Ages and the Renaissance with considerable penetration, and he added such masters of hard-bitten style as Mantegna to his teachers-at-second-hand, with consequent tightening of the often flaccid Pre-Raphaelite style. His *Chant d'Amour* (Plate H11) is a fine Pre-Raphaelite synthesis in which the faults of the movement are minimized, its virtues made the most of. We may be conscious first of the strained medievalism, including the affectation of a French title. But the tapestrylike design, the conscientious craftsmanship, and the effectively nostalgic recall of the age of the troubadours are merits in a painting exemplifying a school that has suffered recently because it runs counter in every way to the aesthetics of today's modernism.

American Romantic Landscape

We have seen that in the painting of men like Peale and Copley America produced an art that paralleled the colonies' cultural relationship to the mother country. As an offshoot of English painting, early American paintings might have been produced in any country similarly settled. But around 1825 there appeared a type of romantic landscape that could have been born nowhere else, not only because the subjects were unique to the American scene but, more importantly, because the painters' response was equally indigenous.

The Hudson River School of painters discovered in the American countryside a half-tamed beauty that had little to do with Constable's richly domesticated scenes, and in the American wilderness a wild but benevolent spirit unrelated to the cosmic symphonies of Turner. The "school" was never an organized one; the term is conveniently applied to a group of two dozen or so painters who, from about 1825 to about 1870, ranged from the Hudson and the Catskills to the Far West. Their work included a large element of fantasy; we have seen an *Imaginary Landscape* (Portfolio 1, Plate 7) by Asher B. Durand (1796–1886) as an example of romantic conception and *In the Catskills* (Portfolio 12, Plate 141) by Thomas Cole (1801–1848) as an example of poetic and visionary art. But Cole's *The Oxbow of the Connecticut River* (*Figure 20*) is more typical of the school as a whole, a jeweled landscape filled with infinite detail and stretching far into exciting and promising distances of a new land that was still opening up and yielding its riches to an enthusiastic and explorative nation.

In its combination of mystery and benevolent richness the country inspired writers as well as painters to reflections upon nature as the revelation of God's love. After Cole's death in 1848, Durand painted *Kindred Spirits* (Plate H12) as his eulogy, showing the painter with his friend, the nature poet William Cullen Bryant, standing on a craggy ledge and con-

templating the kind of wild yet intimate landscape that inspired early nineteenth-century Americans to philosophical musings. Bryant's poetry and, to a certain extent, Cole's and Durand's landscapes are out of fashion today, but if they are marked by a kind of naïveté not popular in the twentieth century, they are also refreshing in their optimism, their conviction of the triumph of good.

Even in the second generation of Hudson River painters, when the relatively mild country of the East had been domesticated and the West was being opened up to reveal an unimaginably vast terrain of mountains, chasms, and deserts, nature remained benevolent rather than menacing in its grandeur, tolerating the infiltration of man rather than begrudging him a place. *The Rocky Mountains* (*Figure 21*) by Albert Bierstadt (1830–1902) might be compared with a Turner to make this point. The Indian camp in the foreground is an Elysium

Figure 20

28

Figure 21

against the majestic background of sun, water, and infinite peak-filled distances. The scene is not an invention but a transcription of one of the scenes Bierstadt saw when he accompanied a surveying expedition into the Rockies and the Yosemite Valley. Thus the picture might be called realistic; but the scene itself is so romantic that it satisfies every requirement of, for instance, the French romantics in their passion for the faraway, the exotic, the savage, the grand, and the mysterious. By a paradox, the illusion sought by Chateaubriand in *Atala*, by Delacroix in his oriental scenes, becomes a reality in the art of a country unconcerned with aesthetic controversies but fascinated with the look of its own romantic self.

29

Color Plates

Figures